HOW I BECAME AN ENGLISHMAN

JOHN PETER

How I Became An
Englishman

As Told to

JUDITH BURNLEY

Salamander Street

First published in 2021 by Salamander Street Ltd.
(info@salamanderstreet.com)

How I Became an Englishman © John Peter and Judith Burnley, 2021

Foreword © Jeremy Irons, 2021

ISBN: 9781913630966

Printed and bound in Great Britain

10 9 8 7 6 5 4 3 2 1

Foreword by Jeremy Irons

Like many actors lucky enough to play noticeable roles in major British theatres, I lived in fear of John Peter and his possible public pronouncements upon my puny efforts. And having a deep seated instinct not to court the critics I would studiously avoid him on occasions when our paths crossed. Only after his retirement, and usually at our annual celebration for the Ian Charleson Awards which he had founded in 1990, did we begin our friendship. And our meetings were always punctuated with frenzied enquiries as to why I hadn't attempted certain roles yet, and, if not, what was I going to do about it.

At the age of sixteen, as a rustic Hungarian, his passion for theatre was born as he watched a production of *Richard III* at the National Theatre in Budapest. He was introduced to the power great writing and great drama could have in society as he experienced the audience's visceral connection to a play written 300 years earlier.

And it was that passionate search for the "real thing" that drove him on in his search for great performances, great productions, and exceptional emerging talent. It was a passion so uncompromising that it sometimes lost him friends in his search for excellence. But it was a passion that never allowed what he considered the second rate to go unrecognised.

This charming memoir, set down by his second wife, the novelist and playwright Judith Burnley, almost in his own words, charts Peter's extraordinary journey from rural poverty in Hungary through the ever present danger of being a Jew, a young revolutionary during the Russian Occupation, his escape to and welcome in the country of his dreams, mastering its language as an Oxford undergraduate as he turned his passion to good use and grew into one of the most respected London Theatre Critics of his time.

1

I t all began with *Richard III*.

The audacious artistic director of The National Theatre in Budapest decided to take advantage of the slight thaw in the icy grip of censorship for a couple of years after Stalin's death in 1953 to put on the most politically provocative of Shakespeare's history plays.

True, the director, Tomas Major, was also a leading actor, and longed to play the wicked King, but all the same, his production was more than a risk: it was an extraordinary show of courage and defiance.

Here was a play about an evil despot who ruthlessly murders anyone who gets in his way, a tyrant who regularly wrote the scripts used to try, find guilty and execute his enemies, just like in the show trials staged in the capitals of the Soviet Block – a recent memory.

Such a play could not have been put on anywhere in Soviet territory while Stalin was alive, and although the easing up in the three years after his death had meant that Hemingway's *The Old Man and the Sea,* which had won the Nobel Prize, and Solzenitsyn's *One Day in the Life of Ivan Denisovitch* could be published in Hungarian, it did not really amount to much: the odd joke might be allowed, the possibility of an occasional pessimistic remark about the human lot, a less fervent singing of those relentlessly optimistic songs about marching into the glorious Soviet future, but Tomas Major was undaunted, and went ahead.

I was sixteen at the time of this event, and living in rural poverty in a village called Dunaföldvár deep in the countryside along the Danube when one of my Godfathers, (eminent Godparents having been dutifully supplied by my parents at my Baptism in the Basilica of St. Stephen where they had been married) invited me to Budapest to see the play. I knew, of course, that my appearance, let alone my lack of manners or social graces would seem shocking in the city: after village school hours I worked with a donkey called Rudi and a rickety cart, collecting water from ancient wells for the local vineyards, and the only clothes I had were shabby, worn out peasant ones, but fortunately, though I knew I would feel mortified by my scruffy appearance, it did not prevent me from accepting this exciting invitation, and attending the play.

I must have known, somehow, that I had to be there, though I could not have predicted that I would be present at one of those rare moments when Art actually influences Society, nor that seeing it do so would shape my future, dictate the priority of Drama in my life, and – subconsciously, of course – my career as theatre critic.

The thousand seat theatre was packed and the audience rapt, bodies taut, faces tense with concentration, only too aware of the parallels between Richard's manipulation of the truth in his drive to power and the recent real-life drama they'd all witnessed: the show trial of the former Minister of the Interior and founder of the ÁVO –

the Hungarian MI5, later to become the Gestapo – László Rajk, when he was tortured until he confessed to crimes against the State he'd never even dreamed of.

Stalin had ordered such trials in every Communist country and the accusations were always the same: the victims had conspired with Western Imperialists in a plot to murder leaders of the Party.

Everyone knew that such accusations were trumped up and completely fake: the trials were scripted dramas – they selected someone from the top, made them read a script detailing their imagined crimes, then executed them, as an example.

Like the drama it was, each trial was completely rehearsed. "Everyone knew their lines," said the current Head of the ÁVO with satisfaction, referring to the Rajk trial. One brave Bulgarian victim had dared to denounce the testimony he was compelled to read. "They tortured me to make me say this," he said. "Not one word of it is true. It's a load of lies." They took him away and tortured him again, until he made the usual, fake, forced confession.

The purpose of all these horrifying charades? To show the country that only The Party had power. That we lived in a One Party State, that power resided only and entirely in that Party, and the Party was embodied only and absolutely in the person of Stalin.

No wonder, therefore that when we reached the point in Shakespeare's play where Richard, Buckingham and their henchmen were manipulating the masses, and faking public support to crown Richard King, the shock of the audience's recognition was palpable. Only Lord Hastings is vociferously opposed, so that when Buckingham asks Richard:

"Now, My Lord, what shall we do if we perceive
Lord Hastings will not yield to our complots?"

and Richard replies: "Chop off his head, man," it would be fair to say the mid-Twentieth Century audience was unusually gripped.

Richard banishes Hastings to the Tower and sends Catesby to kill him. His head is duly delivered in a bloody sack. Then a Scrivener comes on to explain that he has in his hand a paper which is "the indictment of" Richard "by the good Lord Hastings" who has spent the last hours of his "'untainted" life writing it so that it might be read out at St. Paul's that very day, a few hours after his death.

The Scrivener concludes by asking the audience:

"Who is so gross
That cannot see this palpable device?
Yet who's so bold but says he sees it not?"

At this there was a kind of collective gasp and the entire audience rose to their feet and cheered and cheered. Looking round me I was shaken to see a man with tears running down his face and down through his spectacle frames: it was the first time I had seen a grown man cry. We applauded for fully five or six minutes, which felt like a lifetime. I held my breath. Maybe this was it. Revolt! A thrill ran through the theatre like a tidal wave. We were all electrified.

Revolution! It could be here and now. The doors would be flung open and we would all pour out of the theatre, march down the streets to Parliament and depose our own version of an evil monarchy. The will of the people in action.

In the event, however, the Uprising took another year and a bit to happen – October 23rd 1956, a date engraved on all Hungarian hearts. But when it happened, I was in the midst of it. I was there.

2

After this dramatic interlude, however, I had to go back to the countryside – back to Dunaföldvár village school, back to watering the vineyards with my poor little donkey, Rudi, and with Chepi, a small one-eyed pony who had joined us in our chores. But the bleakest return was to an increasingly turbulent domestic life with my mother and stepfather in the tiny one-room house we had built with our own hands with wattle and daub in the primitive manner on a hillside outside the village.

My stepfather, Gery (for Gerard) Prasnovsky was quite a character. His mother was a Frenchwoman from Blois who had married into the minor Hungarian nobility, and accordingly, he had been blessed with a roll-call of illustrious Christian names: Gerard, Dezsos, Henrik, Geza and Pal (or Paul). His father, Count Ivan Prasnovsky, had been Hungarian Ambassador to Paris and Madrid, and was a kind, humorous and highly intelligent man whom I came to love and respect very much, but his son was altogether a different matter. When he first came on the scene, however, I was thrilled to have a father figure in my life, having never accepted or indeed believed in, let alone recovered from the murder of my own beloved father at the hands of Hungarian Nazis in December 1944, when I was six years old. So even though I was now thirteen, I regarded the somewhat mediaeval customs my stepfather demanded of me as a newly acquired son, such as pulling his boots off for him every night, as privileges, though his cuffing me round the head in disgust at my appalling table manners – my mother, being that fashionable thing a 'Free Spirit', had never bothered to teach me any – was more difficult to tolerate.

It was a strange match, I suppose, between the beautiful, head-strong and demandingly modern Veronica and a man bred into centuries of hard-and-fast pre-war eastern European tradition. In fact, it was a marriage which very nearly failed to take place at all when Vera, as she was mostly known, discovered, sometime into their courtship, that Gery was a heavy drinker, and refused to marry him on the grounds that he was an alcoholic. But showing sudden and unexpected strength of character and determination to win her, Gery not only gave up drink, but wooed her with a cunning plan. He very soberly got himself a job at Stalin Varos, one of the new steelworks or Stalin Cities the Brave New World of Communism was developing in remote rural areas, and arranged for the three of us to leave Budapest before we were deported on the back of a truck with a few miserable possessions, to be billeted willynilly on unsuspecting kulaks or peasants with their own houses.

I had had to watch my much-loved grandparents being driven away from Budapest like this not long before. Families like mine were deemed to be class enemies, so they were banished from the city, and their houses and flats taken over with alacrity by party officials.

This prospect was more exciting than daunting to me because, while Russia was turning Hungary from Fascism to Communism, I was turning from an intensely devout little Catholic into a fervent young Stalinist. Looking back, I suppose it was the drama of these two religions which had entranced me: with Catholicism it was the hymns, the stories of the saints, the appalling tragedy of the crucifixion related to us in junior school twice weekly by a good looking young monk; later, with Stalinism it was the flags, the songs, the slogans, the fiery speeches, the electric atmosphere of the constant meetings held to rally the faithful to the Cause. I fantasized that one day dear Uncle Joe would come to my school and I would be chosen to welcome him, and would, of course, make a speech to him he'd never forget.

On Stalin's 70th birthday in 1949 schools were encouraged to fete him, so I wrote a congratulatory letter, and organised my classmates to come up one by one to my desk and sign it. Then I signed it myself with the Russian version of my name:

Ivan Petrov. All this must have been a trial to the grown ups around me. I remember Gery muttering under his breath: "I'll tell you what I wish for HIM on his birthday!" but at the time such remarks went completely over my head.

I was always singing ghastly Commie songs like

> Comrades in the name of Stalin
> Ready for work, now march ahead
> Comrade Rákosi, our people are now
> A solid Bastion.
> Take us along on the road to Victory
> A happy world awaits us.

and writing fervent letters to our President, Comrade Rákosi, our very own Hungarian Stalin. Once my lovely grandma, Illonka Neni, my mother's mother, said: "Look at him, spouting all this stuff", but she seemed merely amused.

Perhaps they knew I'd grow out of it as I learned gradually what Communism was doing to the people around me, but when we went to help build this remote new Stalin City all three of us tried to enter into the spirit of things. Both

Gery and Vera got jobs there, and I went to the make-shift school. It did not take long, however, for reality to set in. Workers at Stalin Varos had to rent rooms in the village of Dunaföldvár, and were taken to work and brought back every day in trucks. This was not a comfortable experience – the trucks were full of dirty, disillusioned men who were even more dirty and disillusioned on the way back when they were tired, hungry, smelly and damp. There was no cover on these trucks, and when it rained, it rained.

Poor Vera had to climb up into the back with the men jeering at her and it was not long before her optimism for the project was eroded by this twice daily ordeal.

It did not take long, however, for both of them to be sacked, for anything that went wrong was naturally blamed on class enemies, and things were always going wrong. A new apartment block had been so hurriedly built it lacked stairs or entrances, and was therefore useless, and as a result of the fury at this cock-up Gery lost his job, Vera left hers, we went back to live in Dunaföldvár, and made a new plan.

Gery, (and after school, I), would get a donkey and cart and take water to the local vineyards. We would sell one or two valuables, buy a piece of land, and build ourselves a house with our own hands. I was full of admiration for Gery's practical knowledge in these matters. He may have been referred to as 'The Count' by our village neighbours but he got things done, charming some of them to help us with the ancient technique of wattle and daub, but building the chimney entirely himself. And not only did his chimney work, but he discovered we could heat the place with a slow burning dust from a textile factory by the river.

To my surprise, I found helping with the wattle and daub most enjoyable, as was the pressing down of the earth around the new walls. While we were working with them, our neighbours also brought us food, which, as we were always hungry, was the most enjoyable thing of all. Later on, Gery improved the seat in the rickety old cart

I had to drive to the vineyards, so it wouldn't be so easy for me to fall out of. Even my mother was impressed.

All went well for a while: I loved the village school which, after the makeshift worker's school in Stalin City seemed like Eton or Winchester, and though our stomachs were always rumbling, there was much laughter amid the hardship in our little house, a lot of it at my expense. I was always writing some epic historical saga, and reading extracts of the latest one of an evening seemed to keep Gery and Vera vastly entertained.

My classmates at school were almost all girls, the Technical Department having claimed the boys, and they quickly became such good friends that I still go back every year for a reunion dinner at which we all revert to our schooldays and laugh and laugh. At this time, however, I was so hungry the girls would share their sandwiches with me, in return for which I did their homework, craftily making a different mistake for each so as not to be caught out.

Watering the vineyards regularly meant that we soon became friendly with the two local wine makers, Uncle Mishka and Uncle Jozsi, so that when my grandfather managed to come and visit us, to witness his grandson in the unlikely role of water-carrier, he who had once had vineyards of his own, made friends with the Uncles, too, and was soon discussing the different crops, the position of each vineyard in relation to sun and wind, and enjoying a stoop or two of wine.

Later, when he was back in Budapest, one of the Uncles sent him a bottle of wine. He sampled it with pleasure, but there was no note with it to say which Uncle it was from. Without hesitation he wrote a note of thanks: he told us he knew immediately he tasted it which vineyard the wine was from. And he was right.

We also had a jocular friendship with a neighbouring farm labourer family of five brothers called Morro who we referred to at home as Spitty Morro, Shitty Morro, Grainy Morro (a miller), and Grapey Morro, who was often so hungry he used to creep into the vineyard, lie on the ground and eat grapes from below.

I was fast becoming a strong young peasant boy, learning to carry heavy loads, earning an extra bob or two by digging up the stubborn roots of Maize plants after the harvest so they could plant the next crop, and lugging some of them home to use as firewood as they burned forever. I even learned how to use that dangerous thing, a Scythe.

It seemed we had settled into this hard, hungry rural life, but then, of course, Gery began to drink again.

This became obvious when he started having accidents driving the cart on the rough country lanes, causing damage to our cart and to the carts or wagons of our neighbours. Sometimes he was unable to untie Rudi and Chepi at the end of the day and see them safely fed and sheltered for the night. One night they fell into a pit and I had the greatest difficulty getting them out in the morning. Sometimes he was too drunk to drive the cart at all and became a noisy, menacing presence in the tiny house. Naturally, we kept on running out of money – I can remember my mother actually crying with hunger once – and they had terrible rows which I tried, unsuccessfully not to hear. But the drinking continued.

Round about the same time, I began to have a breakdown of my own: stories began to leak out about terrible beatings up and torture of those who, somehow, failed to toe the Stalinist line. I tried to ignore all this, until one day I heard about a man I'd known and liked in Stalin City, a friend of Gery's in his late fifties who'd always been very nice to me. It seemed he had complained about something trivial and this had been taken as a sign of disloyalty to the Party. He had been beaten until he'd pissed blood. I broke down, kicking the wall and screaming and ending up huddled in a heap on the floor in a serious state of mental and spiritual breakdown. I'd lost my second religion and it seemed there was nothing in the world left to believe in.

Both Vera and Gery were sympathetic, in their way, but there was little they could do. Gery was generally too drunk to help anyone, and Vera too preoccupied in trying to cope with him, and making plans for she and I to leave. They were both supportive, though, when I decided I would like to have religious education at school – a desperate attempt, I suppose, to find something to believe in. Religion was, of course, banned by the Soviet, but there was a loop hole whereby if twelve pupils demanded it, the school could go ahead. Unsurprisingly, however, never more than eleven were found. This was probably just as well because had I been allowed this instruction, a black mark would have gone down in my records and I would have been banned from going to university, and from many professions. Indeed, it was a considerable risk even to ask for it, and brave of Vera and Gery to condone me doing so.

Meanwhile, Gery's drinking was causing more and more problems, and things came to a head one day when he took my father's typewriter, a sacred object to me, as was anything connected with my father, and a valuable one to my mother, intending to sell it to buy the necessities of life. On his return, however, he showed my mother a paltry sum and it was clear he had drunk most of the money away. This was the last straw, and we left that night, abandoning Gery (and poor little Rudi and Chepi) to their fate.

Back in Budapest, we were put up in the flat of some friends of Vera's who worked for the Department of Education, and through them I was suddenly thrown into the highly competitive milieu of the Westminster or St. Paul's of Budapest, the best boys' school in a city of intellectuals. So here was I, with my peasant's clothes and uncouth manners, used to being the cleverest boy in the girl's school, confronted by sixth form boys who quoted Pascal in class, a thinker I'd never even heard of. After nearly four years in Dunaföldvár I was badly shaken by this sudden change, but I suppose I must have gradually adjusted. I made friends I still have to this day, and by the time the uprising happened, less than a year later, I was in there with the rest.

3

It was in the Sixth form of this school that we heard from some old boys now at University that something significant was about to happen. It seems that some brave and enlightened young people had been planning rebellion for years, not surprising since by 1956 Hungary had been under the Stalinist yoke for a decade, and they had drawn up a list of freedoms which they wanted to demand from the government by broadcasting them to the nation from the central radio station.

The rebellion was planned to start with a seemingly harmless demonstration, but to hold a demonstration you had to apply to the authorities for permission, and this could take years. Now, however, they had been given the go-ahead to gather at the foot of the statue of Polish General Józef Benn, who had won a victory for us in 1848. This must have seemed harmless enough to the authorities, who had not been informed that we were actually demonstrating solidarity with contemporary intellectuals in Poland who were under pressure to conform to the Soviet way of life.

The university students who gave us this news warned us, that, as we were still at school it was absolutely forbidden for us to join in. This warning naturally made us all the more eager to do so, and I think the entire sixth form was there. How that meeting developed into a major uprising is a matter of history.

The idea was to get the crowd at the 1848 memorial ceremony to march through town with them to the radio station, cheering them onwards. And so we all began to march in a joyfully rebellious mood. Then Hungarian flags started to appear at windows, many of them with a big hole cut out of the middle where the hated Soviet emblem, the hammer and sickle, had been cut out. As we went on, more and more people were leaning out to cheer us on, and, even better, joining us in the streets.

It was not long, however before the ÁVO, the Hungarian Gestapo got wind of what was up, and started shooting into the crowd.

I remember it was late afternoon, just beginning to get dark, and I was in a large crowd standing in front of the Parliament building when a Hungarian truck came across the square and put up two flags which had great bloodstains on them, so we all knew, everyone knew, there were wounded people in that truck they were trying to take to hospital, people the ÁVO had shot at.

A man who must surely have been an electrician was climbing up to the spire of the cathedral and cutting off the Red Star alight on top of it. He brought it down and displayed it and we, the crowd, cheered like mad.

There was an awkward moment for me while we were marching down the boulevards when I suddenly saw my mother outside the little button shop where she worked. She was beckoning me to leave the march and come in, but I simply crossed my arms in an emphatic 'NO', and carried on.

The atmosphere was electric. For quite a lot of the way I must have been very conspicuous: I was sitting in the front of a truck, high up in the air on the bonnet shouting: 'Work and Bread for us, and the noose for Rákosi', (a version of a WW2 anti-Nazi slogan), but I had no idea I was in any danger. By the time we got to the radio station they were using tear gas on us and I got a dose of it. It was not a pleasant experience.

Violence was all around us, but one scene I can never get out of my mind is the image of a young country boy about my age, with a round face and fresh cheeks, sitting on a truck with blood running down his face from his head. He had been hit by stones because he was in Soviet uniform, clearly having been conscripted into the Red Army to do his National Service. Many boys were sent to the ÁVO rather than the Army – they had no choice – and they knew while there, and in that uniform, that everyone would hate them. Even in the best of times, Hungarians never liked the Police. I was wondering what I could do to help this boy when a man next to me went on to the truck, put his hand on the boy's shoulder and said: "There, there, my boy, it's not you we want, it's the bastards who put you here".

It was quite a problem to get through the crowd to the huge main doors of the Radio HQ, and even more of a problem to get through the doors themselves. I was in a group helping to push a van hard enough to ram it through the heavy doors, an exercise which nearly lost me most of the fingers of my right hand: they'd got jammed for a nasty few moments in the van door.

All this was well worthwhile, however, as, eventually, we broke down the door, the student activists managed to get in and their carefully worded demands of freedom for the Hungarian people were broadcast to the Nation.

It was not until one of my recent visits to the site of the radio station, walking down that street nearly sixty years later, that I realised that so many young men and boys had been killed around me. There was so much going on that we simply didn't notice young bodies falling around us, so I was shocked to see a new plaque that had been put up a foot or so behind where I had been standing, to another Janos of exactly my age, which was just eighteen. And another to several boys just a little older, who, like the boy on the truck, had been conscripted into the Red Army on National Service to fight for the hated regime and had switched to the Revolutionary side, only to be shot by their own former colleagues. I knew that one of my classmates had been so badly wounded in the thigh he had lived all his life as a cripple, but these boys had lost their lives.

Now, I saw a new plate glass building called Magyar Radio behind the old one, overlooking the autumnal park surrounding the classical building of the History Museum. We were in a new century, and as I walked beneath the trees through those elegantly styled grounds, it was only autumn leaves that fell around me.

Hungarian life changed forever in those crucial moments in 1956 on these still gracious streets, and so did mine. From now on, my life would have to be elsewhere, though I did not come to realise this for five or six weeks after the event.

The rest of that momentous day and the day after became a blur. Groups of us wandered about, only half aware of the danger we were in, wondering what had actually happened. I suppose we were in a state of shock. The fierce Magyar spirit had risen up against the tyrants, and the urge to freedom had – for a few hours – overcome the fear of the reprisals which were sure to come. What, if anything, had we won? Had we changed anything? What would happen now?

Some people were joyfully dismantling the giant bronze statue of Stalin and putting Hungarian flags in his boots. Others were shoved into trucks and never seen again. There was random gunfire, and beatings up, and I am ashamed to say that the gunfire frightened me. I had not yet done my National Service, so had not learned how to handle a gun and shoot back.

I was outside the huge art nouveau apartment building at the foot of the Elizabeth Bridge where my schoolfriend Fery lived, (and still lives to this day), when I heard someone call my name. Fery's mother was leaning out of the window signalling frantically for me to come up out of danger. So (cowardly, I regret to say) I did, and I stayed with Fery for two or three days, after which I found a bus stop and went back to the suburb where I had been staying with my Aunt Judka, arriving with the information that, because there was an armament factory in her neighbourhood, people leaving the area would be arrested.

Most of the activists and people who'd participated, left the country immediately after the uprising, helped in their risky attempts to cross the border with Austria by the fact that rebels sympathetic to our cause had destroyed some of the barricades. At that point, however, I had not yet realised that my life in Hungary was over. I was in a kind of trance in which the kind of house arrest I found myself in suited me. I never went back to school again, and I quickly sank into a kind of limbo in which the future was unknowable, and only the very peculiar life I'd lived up to then seemed real to me.

4

The reprisals were swift, fierce and prolonged, so that people began to long to return to the old oppressive life they regarded as normal. As for me, I had never known a 'normal' life. Until I was two I had been the pampered baby of a wealthy and much respected family, and spoiled and cooed over in particular by my father's father, the formidable Eugene Peter, head of Franklin, Budapest's most prestigious and internationally renowned book publishing house. My grandfather's plan was that, after him, my father would run the show (somewhat reluctantly, since he wanted to continue his career as a much respected Art Historian), and after him, it would be me. Meanwhile, I was indulged in every whim in a new house my parents had organised around me, and especially in Eugene's (or Yentzi kem, as we called him) grand house, pandered to by his servants. This may explain why my mother, the young, wilful and handsome Veronica (Vera), who liked to describe herself as that fashionable thing 'a free spirit', decided to leave my father, (and his so dominating father), and take two-year-old me with her.

No one has ever understood why she did this, but with hindsight I think the fuss they all made of me might have been the cause. Once I'd been born and she'd produced the necessary heir, no one had time for her anymore. She was used to being the centre of attention: she had been a (not very successful) actress before she married, and I suspect that she didn't at all like being relegated to the role of the lucky mother of me. She had not the remotest inclination or talent for motherhood, had no idea of a baby or a child's needs, and avoided, as much as possible, looking after me. She should, really, have made her escape and left me behind, but she felt the Peter family had bruised her ego, she wanted to hurt them back, and she knew the best way to do that was to rob them of me.

In this she succeeded beyond her wildest dreams. My father went into a depression, and my grandfather started a law case against her which went on acrimoniously from 1940 for most of the war years. Finally, late in 1944, it was agreed that she could have me until I was six, and then she must return me to my father and his family. It has been the tragedy of my life that, just after I turned six, my father was captured by the ÁVO, arrested and probably tortured, then marched, with other undesirables across the Chain Bridge, taken down the steps to the Danube, shot in the back and pushed into the river.

This could only have happened in the last six weeks of 1944, for at the beginning of the war President Horty had done a deal with the Nazis that Budapest Jews would not be rounded up, though this did not exempt those living elsewhere. From May 1944, however, the Germans became aware, if not quite consciously, that they might not win the war. The main theatre of war moved out of Hungary, Horty lost power and Hitler, anxious to fulfil as much as possible of the Thousand Year Reich's policy of extermination, the Final Solution, moved his hardened hitman Adolf Eichmann's Headquarters to Budapest.

Holing up in one of the most luxurious hotels in central Budapest, Eichmann set about this task with zeal, and by July 1944 he had sent 440,000 Hungarian Jews, dissidents, and other undesirables, to Auschwitz-Birkenau, almost all of whom died.

My father was not among them. He survived until December, but seemed to have something of a fatalistic streak and did not take too much trouble to hide. He was living, then, with a remarkable woman called Magda, planning to marry her, (it was my good fortune to get to know and love Magda some thirty years on), and it is possible that the happiness he had with her may have given him a false sense of security, for he used to stand at their open door to greet visitors without worrying who would see him. At the same time, he was given to making remarks to his sister Mitzi like: "I shan't survive this".

Little Janos.

With his adored father, Andras.

With his mother, Veronica.

Oxford undergraduate.

Tea with Colonel, Mrs. Simons and Elizabeth in their garden. JP second from left.

Rowing in the college team at Oxford. JP second left.

Ticking off Judi Dench.

Retire? They must be joking.

She did not take him seriously, though, as it was a family joke that he had always been fond of making dramatic utterances of this kind.

So it was in this period at the end of 1944 when Soviet tanks were already approaching our Border, planning to liberate us from one tyranny only to put us immediately under another, that the ÁVO outdid themselves in hunting down dissidents and undesirables of every kind, imprisoning them, torturing them, and beating them up, before killing them in the nastiest way they could think of.

Every time I go to Budapest I go down those steps and stand at the river's edge, where he was pushed in, but I have never been able to make myself walk across The Chain Bridge. At the same time, I have never been able to convince myself that he was really dead.

I had not got over the loss of my father's presence in my daily life when, at two years old, Vera took me away from him, but at least I knew he was there somewhere, and I would get to see him when I could. Perhaps that is why I could never bring myself to believe I would never see him again, and am haunted by so many recurring dreams.

In one, he appears in a dazzling white light in a white suit with a white suitcase on his shoulder, and beckons me to follow him, but when I turn to do so, he vanishes. Another is that he had been washed up downriver, undead: that he'd been found and rescued and was living in some remote part of the countryside, full of forests and deep Danube bends. It is hard to bear, this dream, this undying hope. Have I failed him? Should I try to find him? Perhaps he's still waiting for me, as I am waiting, still, for him. In the last dream I can remember I was told I could find him by the steps to the Danube where he'd been killed, and I flew through the air along the riverside to join him, seeing all the buildings, the sights he would have seen on the way there, for the last time, himself. But when I got there, there was something wrong. I could feel it. "It's not you, is it?", I said. And he shook his head. "No, it's not me," he said.

In the period after Vera took me away, I was often sent to live in nurseries or childcare homes, and later, as the war progressed, hidden in convents and monasteries for a safety I didn't know I needed, a situation which sometimes provided Vera with opportunities to be a Drama Queen. I remember once, when I'd been in a convent for about six weeks, she appeared, knelt on the floor and opened her arms for me to run into them while the nuns looked on. I must admit, however, that whenever I was living with her she must have been driven mad by my asking her all the time when I would see Papa.

She never told me he was dead, and I simply thought that, like other boys' fathers, he had gone away to the war, so I waited on street corners, and at bus stops, in front of windows and doors, running after trams, sometimes, when I thought I'd seen him. Other boys' fathers had come back. Why not mine?

I suppose Vera simply didn't know what to say or how to tell me, but I think now that she felt guilty that she had been responsible for his death. My grandfather certainly thought so, and accused her of it. He knew that Bundy, (my father's nickname – he was Andras and it was like Andy for Andrew) would have left the country if it had not been for wanting, even if only occasionally, to see me. Ironically, Bundy had had plans early in the marriage to take up an art historian's post at the Warburg Institute in London. He had friends there, and the eminent art historian James Pope Henessy had published an essay of his in *The Burlington Magazine*, so he went to London before the war, and put £2000 in a British bank thinking we would all three go and live there. Strange to think that, if that had happened, I would probably have ended up at Oxford anyway, (though my early life would have been rather less eventful!)

This plan was of course, foiled by Vera's leaving, though I doubt if she'd have agreed to go, anyway, but she must have known that Bundy would not have been killed if he had not stayed in a Budapest that was not safe for him, simply because I was there.

I had no idea until I was seventeen why it was unsafe for Bundy to stay in Budapest, or why it was necessary to hide me in convents and monasteries for so much of my early childhood. I had been brought up as a devout little Catholic, my parents had married in the Basilica of St. Stephen, and I had been baptised there. My cousins Imre and Ishti went to the best Catholic Boys' School, and it was only when I was seventeen, and half – listening to a conversation between Gery and Vera that I heard something that puzzled me. "What are you talking about?" I asked them. "Who in the family is Jewish?" "Everyone," said my mother carelessly. So I did that thing one does in moments of shocked incomprehension, saying "What!? And Aunt Judka? And Uncle so and so? And then with a shock, I realised, and I said: "Is that why he died?"

It seemed that, like so many well to do Budapest families, my grandfather had converted in order to get on and to be part of the society around him. Budapest then was very much like New York in many ways: people lived in flats in tall buildings along wide boulevards and went down to the street for a regular coffee and some patisserie, the intelligentsia were disproportionately Jewish, and words like 'mishbuka' (extended family) had gone into the language, so I had no idea they were not Hungarian. But I had no idea of our background, and it was probably quite sensible not to tell me while I was at school during the Nazi period. To prove that you were not Jewish to the Nazis you had to have four Christian grandparents.

During the years of my mother's custody I never had a real home or a proper meal, and I was taught nothing except how to wash up, and polish her shoes. Once she sent me to the Gas Board to explain why she couldn't pay the bill. I think I was eight. They let her off the bill, but said, severely, "Please don't send your little boy again," which made her laugh. When I wasn't being left in a nursery, or hidden in a convent, we lived in a series of rented rooms and she was mostly out at whatever work she could find. I slept with the light on, I was forbidden to play with other children or to invite friends or neighbours in to play with me. At weekends, however, I was allowed to visit both sets of grandparents – a wonderful contrast, as I loved them all, and they loved me. My maternal grandparents always made a traditional Sunday lunch for all the family: this was my only taste of normal family life and I relished it. My two close cousins, Imre and Ishti were made to help with the washing up, but I, as the youngest, sat on my grandpapa, Bela Baci's lap and played with his watch chain while he smoked his pipe.

These moments were in stark contrast to the dangers I was often in without knowing it. There was the time when I was taken to a new convent and left there, and I cried so much they couldn't pacify me. The Mother Superior knew it wasn't safe to contact either of my parents so, in desperation, she managed to find my Aunt Mitzi, Bundy's sister, who was married to a respected Viennese lawyer so had some freedom of movement, and she came to fetch me. That night the convent was raided by the Gestapo and all the children taken off and killed.

Another time I was found wandering along the street in a feverish daze by my Peter grandparents. "Just look at this child," cried my grandmother. "He's got a temperature. Must be measles or mumps. Out at all times in the street, alone." She broke down and wept. Together they took me home to the current bedsit, managed somehow to get in, undressed me tenderly, found some pyjamas in a cupboard, tucked me up in bed, kissed me better, and left.

When Vera came home and heard it was they who had put me to bed, she was furious. She leaned over me threateningly – the wicked witch in *Snow White* – screaming at me, her face close to mine. "Don't you know they hate me? They hate your sweet Mama." (Mummy in Hungarian translates as 'sweet mother'). They say terrible things about me. They say I killed Papuka. They say I was responsible for his death." I started to cry. "He's not dead," I sobbed. "He's coming back for me, I know he is."

I don't suppose that Vera had entirely stopped caring for Bundy, though she might have pretended to herself that she had. She must have been in a very conflicted state. Once we were at war, people were constantly being taken away to camps where they had to do weeks of hard manual labour and from which they returned haggard and hollow eyed. These were not concentration camps – not yet – but punishment camps. I remember one incident when I was about five: Vera was in a telephone box and I was waiting for her in the street outside. It was summer, and very hot, and it seemed to me I was always waiting for her, and always mystified as to why. She was talking to her best friend Magda, and seemed to be agitated in a way that alarmed me. She pushed the door open so I heard: "Magda, it's hot – goodbye". Then she came out crying and shaking, tears running down her face. I was frightened. I had never seen her like this before. There were no explanations, no comfort, no forthcomings. Looking back, I realise that she'd just heard Papuka had been taken away to a camp, and she knew what that would mean for him. Some years later I heard from a friend of his who had been with him at that camp that they had been forced to sleep outside all night chained to a fence, and that Bundy had got through this ordeal by saying 'Janos', my name, over and over again.

The day following this telephone box incident Vera was due to meet Magda at a coffee house, but cancelled the arrangement. The coffee house was in a building that had been badly bombed, and that afternoon it collapsed, and Magda, like everyone in it, was killed.

It seems my childhood consisted of one form of escape or another, but now, having taken part in an historic revolt, I was stuck with my Aunt in the suburbs in a kind of limbo with no idea that the greatest escape of all lay ahead.

5

I think I was finally shocked out of my lethargy by one of our neighbours, a man I knew well and trusted, who came and told us the nature of the Soviet reprisals taking place around us. "They're picking up chaps at random from the street," he said. "They're throwing them into trucks. Those men will never be seen again." I went to the window, saw what he said was true, and knew then that I had to go.

I got into town and went to see my mother at the button shop where she worked. It took half an hour to convince her she had to leave, too. I knew what a miserable life she would have if she stayed in Budapest, and I hadn't the heart to condemn her to it. She was not easy to persuade, but somehow I managed it. There was never any doubt in my mind about where we would go. The place that spoke Freedom to us was England.

It was not only that I knew my father had had plans to go there, or even that, by now, I had not only seen Shakespeare's *Richard III*, but also Laurence Olivier's films of *Henry V* and *Hamlet*. (I had had the instructive experience of seeing *Hamlet* in a barn in the countryside surrounded by men clad head to toe in giant sheepskins, who, as the plot thickened, muttered to each other, tensely: "No good will come of this!'), but had been severely ticked off more than once by whichever aunt I was currently staying with for lurking around on the steps of the British Embassy and trying to peep inside. One could be arrested, then, for standing near or under a foreign flag.

One memorable time I got inside and saw the picture of the young, beautiful Queen who was married to a sailor. I had expected this unlikely consort to look like Yves Menton playing a matelot, and was somewhat surprised by the tall, elegant figure by the Queen's side.

Now I started making plans for myself and my mother, but after a few days she announced that Gery was coming with us. She had no intention of going back to him, though he was still hoping she would. In any case, his intention was to go to Blois in Northern France where his French mother had a house, and he knew we were bound for England, but she clearly thought we needed a man on this expedition. This infuriated me. I was eighteen years old, had just come out the other side of a dangerous uprising and considered myself man enough. I would have been even angrier if I had realised what the old goat was up to.

We were to make the first part of the journey by train, but when we got to the station, we found Gery with his current girlfriend and her eleven-year-old daughter. He had brought them with him in case Vera refused to come back to him. How could he envisage travelling womanless into France? To her credit, my mother did not make a scene, but a cloud settled over the enterprise all the same. The two strangers were hung about with baggage, when it was essential to travel light. I carried only a paper bag with the two volumes of the German edition of my father's book on the first thousand years of Hungarian art, written when he was twenty-four and still being taught in universities today, plus the one spare shirt I owned. Vera took little more. She had pawned the family silver, monogrammed with the cursive NV for Nagy Veronica, and given the ticket to her best friend Ergy (Elizabeth) who had, apparently, lost it. My cousin Imre also joined us at the station, so altogether it was a strange little party that boarded that train.

It was not a comfortable journey. Gery irritated my mother by getting sentimental about a girl sitting opposite who was feeding her baby, and irritated me by insisting I should come to France with him, rather than to England, and go to the Sorbonne rather than Oxford. Both of us were also irritated by his girlfriend making strange clanking noises when she moved. We were to find out the cause of this later.

At a village about half way to the border the train terminated, and here Imre had a change of mind. He felt he could not leave his mother, my Aunt Judka, alone with Uncle Mishka, his pig of a father to mistreat her. I was not to see Imre for twenty-two years, 1978 being the first time it felt safe enough to venture back. Not entirely safe, however. There was a nasty edge to the Passport Controller's voice as he thumbed through my much-used British Passport: "Well, Mr. Peter, you haven't visited us for a very long time," he said. "Was that because you didn't want to, or because you didn't dare to?" This did nothing to make me feel welcome in my homeland.

We got off the train at a small country station from where we had to hitch rides on carts, or trucks to the house of some of Gery's trusty family retainers, and there we were to stay the night and plan the route to the Austrian border. The vital question was where was the least dangerous place to cross. By now, the authorities had refortified the border with gun posts and lookouts and we knew it was going to be hard going. Our hosts put us up in a large barn with one huge bed, and it was here that Vera and I watched with amazement as the Other Woman unstrapped piece after piece of heirloom cutlery from her waist before getting into bed. No wonder she had clanked. Unlike Vera, she had not pawned the family silver.

The following morning we set out for the next village en route and discovered a huge hay wagon being piled up with hay in which we thought we could hide some of the way. There, we met up with other refugees who had the same idea, among them a trio of musicians, Ivan, Tibor and a lovely Gypsy called Janezi. "We've got enough here for a game of cards," joked Gery. We had a heated discussion about which was the best way to the Border – everyone had their own idea, which was not encouraging – then the old man who was piling more hay on the cart warned us that we must climb right up to the top of the wagon to be above bayonet level. "There are Gestapo on the bridge," he said, "and they stick bayonets into the middle."

It wasn't easy to climb up, especially for those with the family cutlery clanking round their waists, but somehow we all managed it. Then we had to pull the straw over our heads so as to be hidden from the road. The wagon then started off, lurching alarmingly along the rough country road and we all tried not to fall out. Poor Ivan, who was the drummer in the trio, got a straw up his nose and had to fight the intense desire to sneeze, which might have unbalanced the lot of us.

We had been told that the wagon would take us as far as a wooden bridge over a small river, and we would have to get off there. Hidden in the straw, we couldn't see anything, but I could tell when we were on the bridge by the sound of the wheels on the wooden structure, and one by one, we all got off. We crossed the bridge on foot and came to another village where we had to wait until dark before moving on. The villagers were a mix of curious, suspicious and sympathetic, but one woman invited us in and gave us food and a local man explained that we had to go up a hill, down the other side, and then we would come to a crossroads which marked the line between Hungary and Austria. I remember this man standing in the doorway of his house looking at us sadly. "Don't go, good people. This is your land," he said, which made me want to cry.

In the event, his directions, like so many of the others, turned out to be wrong. It was dark when we reached No Man's Land, and difficult to see anything, let alone which way to go. I had been planning to chart our course by the stars, having rehearsed the position of the North Star to the Plough, but I was foiled by a cloudy night, so now I looked left and right in consternation. I was going to have to make a fateful decision.

Across the border to the left there was night and silence; to the right cars with lights could be seen moving along lit roads. "We go that way", I said, pointing to the right, knowing that where there was light and movement must be the West, and feeling sure that Communist guerrillas lurked in the darkness on the left, ready to shoot. But Gery disagreed with me, and started a heated argument. Our lives hung in the balance. I lost my temper – for the first and last time in my life, to excellent purpose. "We're going this way!" I shouted. And we did.

We walked for about half an hour and reached a small stream – our Rubicon – over which was a small, clean, beautifully crafted bridge – a Western bridge. We walked across it and saw a man on the other side who Gery greeted in French. The man replied in German. Austria! We were safe. We had done it. We were free. I sat down on a stone by the wayside and cried. No one thanked me for getting it right, but what did that matter? I now had an unknown future spreading out before me.

We walked on in the dark until we came to an Austrian village with lighted shops and people bustling in the street. My mother spoke German, and soon we were led to the village hall where we sat down and were served soup and some very nice food, then we were shown where we could sleep on great sacks filled with straw in a school building. It was clear that people in the villages along the border had helped many refugees like ourselves. The Red Cross played an important part in this, and instructed that refugees should be got away from the border as quickly as possible, so next morning we were set on our way to Linz where offices had been set up to help Hungarians travel to their chosen destinations.

We were put on a bus which took us to a deserted hotel in the mountains where we were shown into an empty bedroom, and my mother and I were just preparing to sleep, when an Austrian guard came in, said something loudly in German and left the room. "What did he say?" I asked my mother. She shrugged. "Oh, only that if anyone here wanted to go to England, get up and raise your hand – there is a bus leaving tomorrow morning." "Then why on earth didn't you?" I shouted. I leapt to my feet and ran after him shouting 'Yah, Yah!"

Next morning, we boarded the bus and there was a pathetic scene where Gery ran alongside it, gesticulating wildly to my mother to get off and come with him. He was crying. Vera turned her profile austerely away, and that was the last we, either of us, saw of him.

We heard many alarming stories on that bus. Not long before, two turncoat ÁVO men had been spotted trying to escape, but had been recognised by two genuine refugees. The ÁVO men had made the mistake of wearing their long leather stormtrooper overcoats, and sinister expressions. The Austrian Authorities promptly sent them back across the border. It was a long journey, and everyone on the bus was hungry, and I remember a giant, a well-known heavyweight wrestler who later became famous in England, gently feeding a small boy with the remains of an orange.

Eventually, we got to Linz, which, like Vienna, had become an organised centre from which Hungarians could be helped to go to their chosen destinations. Western European countries may not have intervened to help us in the uprising, but they were very sympathetic to the cause of those who'd had to leave. Particularly England. We had made it harder for ourselves by leaving our escape so late. Those who had left immediately after the uprising had found things much easier: border barricades had been broken down by sympathisers, and young Englishmen like Christopher Ralling, later of the BBC, had driven borrowed trucks and vans to the border to rescue people.

Oxford and Cambridge Universities sent representatives to Vienna, which was the centre for the refugee crisis, to offer suitable youngsters places at their colleges. Every College had agreed to take one Hungarian student free. By the time I got to England, however, almost all of these places had been taken up, and it was only through the intervention of my new English friends, Colonel and Mrs. Simons, that I got into Campion Hall, more about which anon.

When we got to Linz we were taken to a small plane for England, but this had to land in Germany on the way to refuel and we were fed at the airport canteen. This was an astonishing experience: I had never seen a room full of large men stuffing themselves like this before.

Eventually, we landed at a small light aircraft aerodrome established in 1944 by the US Army on Salisbury Plain, and we came down the plane steps to be welcomed by Womens' Institute Ladies with cups of tea. This turned out to be a thick brown liquid unlike anything we knew as tea, and some of my compatriots were suspicious.

They sniffed it warily, muttering that it didn't look like tea to them, whereupon Vera quelled them with a look. "In England they always put milk in tea," she explained. (In Hungary you only had tea with milk if you were unwell.)

It was only when I'd settled in England and got used to English ways that I realised the significance of that supremely English gesture. The sympathy behind it. The simple kindness. When people have been through untold dangers, when they are suffering from shock or what we now call Post Traumatic Stress Syndrome (PTSD), you offer them a cup of tea.

After this traditional welcome we were put on buses and taken to army barracks near the village of Tidworth where we were fed what seemed to us a superb meal, then shown to dormitories where we were to sleep. We would stay there for a couple of weeks acclimatisation, they explained, and then be moved to another place where we would be helped to find jobs or, in the case of youngsters like myself, university places.

I couldn't believe my ears. We were even to be given pocket money while at Tidworth: ten shillings a week. These people had thought of everything. England was even more wonderful than I'd heard. I went to bed that night and slept soundly for the first time since the uprising on October 23rd. I felt safe. It was now December 19th. Soon it would be Christmas, and my new life was about to begin.

Next morning, I awoke early, had a magnificent breakfast, and went out to explore. On the parade ground outside flew the Union Jack, and, instinctively, I avoided getting too near to it. I'd been warned so many times that to do so was dangerous. Then, suddenly, the penny dropped. I was not in Hungary, where everything was dangerous. I was here. The Union Jack was the symbol of my new home. One day, if all went well, it would be my flag, too.

Vera very quickly regained her imperious great lady manner, but people seemed amused or charmed by it, rather than exasperated. She was so thrilled by the copious amounts of food on offer that she sometimes went back for more as many as four times and this did occasion comment, and amused but not unkind references to *Oliver Twist*. A few days after our arrival it was Christmas Day and we were treated to all the traditional, and to us, eye-opening, revelries and a truly sumptuous Christmas Feast.

It was sometime before I could appreciate the irony of our timing: the barracks at Tidworth were free for us to use because the regiments stationed there were at Suez. So, while the British were rescuing refugees from Soviet tyranny, they were also having a last stab at Imperialism. It was like something out of one of Shakespeare's complex last plays.

I knew two words of English when I came to England: "Cowboy", and "Times". I have no idea how I'd picked up "Cowboy" as we were not allowed corrupt Western films of any kind, let alone those known as "Westerns", but I'd heard that "Times" was the name of the greatest newspaper in the world. Little did I know that I would work for that very newspaper, as well as the *Times Educational Supplement* and most importantly, *The Sunday Times*, for forty years, and it seems ironic now that the way I set about teaching myself English was by trying to read *The Times* every day. Fortunately, I had the help of an Anglo-Hungarian dictionary my mother had acquired for me: she had written for help to a Hungarian she knew was living here and in reply he had sent her the dictionary. Not the kind of help she'd hoped for, but invaluable to me.

Even more helpful, however, was the appearance of a young graduate who was to give us English lessons. He was called Christopher, and was hardly older than myself, but had patience beyond his years. I took to him at once, and I observed with an interest more like envy his grey flannels and worn tweed sports coat. High minded young graduates also came to talk to us about employment, impressing on us that the most important thing was to to get a job and be self-supporting, and we were regularly visited by ladies from the local Women's Institutes who tried to help us find our way forward.

Vera exerted all her charm on these women – she knew a little English and could converse with those who spoke French or German – and this is how she met and we became lifelong friends with the Simons family. Colonel and Mrs. Simons were Catholics, like ourselves, and this cemented the friendship. Their house was the first English house I'd visited, and we soon got to know their son and their daughter, Elizabeth. She is the same age as me, and she and I remain good friends to this day. I have photographs of us having tea in their garden, a quintessentially English scene.

The trio of musicians we'd met in the haystack were with us at Tidworth and we shared some amusing moments of acclimatisation. They were, of course, busy finding out about the music scene here, and did, in fact, become quite successful, playing in a club near Marble Arch where I used to visit them. But early on, at Tidworth, I remember them hearing Victor Silvester being played nostalgically on a gramophone and saying to each other "Goodness, if that's where they're at, we're made!"

With them, and my ten shillings pocket money, I ventured into the village of Tidworth to sample the wicked delights of the West. We sat at a café table and ordered Coca Cola. This drink was, in Soviet dominated States, the most forbidden of all forbidden fruits, the most potent symbol of the decadence of Capitalism. It was thought to contain cocaine, and we wondered why our innocent-looking teenage waitress was allowed to serve it. We sipped, and waited for 'a high'. Time passed and our mood remained unchanged. We were no longer elated, never mind high. Another Capitalist myth exploded.

I had been similarly nonplussed by seeing a magazine with Elvis Presley on the cover and the Headline: Is Elvis a Genius? In Hungary geniuses were grave old gentlemen who looked like the Abbé Lizst in his dotage. How could this half-naked and impossibly gaudy young person be a genius?

After two weeks we were moved to Fleet, in Hampshire, then, later to London where we were put up in a disused church in, of all places, Wapping. Years later I pointed out this church to a colleague from the window of News International where I was working on *The Sunday Times*. "Well, you haven't come very far then," she said.

My first job was in a milk bar in Regent Street at the Langham Place, BBC end, now the site of an All Bar One. We served food I had never heard of, let alone seen or eaten: baked beans on toast, toad in the hole. "Hey, boy!" yelled an outraged American. "Call this a hamburger!?" I had no idea what he was talking about. My next job was a step up: packing up books for schools for the Educational Department of Foyles Bookshop in Charing Cross Road. Here

I encountered a character called Foskett who referred to Sophocles as Soff O'kkells, told me that his missus was called Maud and that Tennyson had written a poem about her called "Come into the garden, Maud", and that for dinner, he always "'ad 'ot jam for afters. I f…..ing loves it," he said.

Altogether I suppose it was a very confusing time. I remember being completely fazed when I'd asked a man in a shop for something and he replied: "We haven't got it, so I'm afraid I can't help you there". This was a puzzle: why was he afraid?

I was obviously at the very beginning of a steep learning curve, but in spite of my greenness, Colonel and Mrs. Simons had decided that I was the kind of boy who should go to Oxford. By this time, most of the Oxford and Cambridge colleges had filled the free places they had allotted to suitable youngsters from Hungary, but the Simons' were not daunted. They sought the help of Father Baines, Chaplain of their local Catholic church, and sure enough, he had access to Father Thomas Corbishley, Master of

Campion Hall, the Jesuit college in Oxford, and arranged an interview for me. As I was convinced that I hadn't got a chance, I was not at all scared. My mother suggested that I go armed with the two black volumes of my father's history of Hungarian Art, then she and I and Mrs. Simons set out towards the dreaming spires.

In the event, it was my father's book which clinched the matter. Father Corbishley was looking at the black and white photograph of a painting of The Ascension, and turning the book to me, asked me what was going on in this painting, and where the figures floating skywards in it were going. "Oh," I said, "They're going up. Up to…" – then I realised I didn't know the word for "Heaven". I froze, gulped and probably turned bright red in my embarrassment as I wracked my brains. There was a tense pause, then I managed: "They are going up – to – to where God lives." My mother and Mrs. Simons have been convinced ever since that this answer is what got me in to Oxford.

The deal at Campion Hall was that I would help out in the kitchen, serve at table, and do sundry odd jobs in return for my education. This seemed fair enough to me and I very much enjoyed my tasks, especially when I learned to shock the good Jesuits by calling their cheese by the Hungarian word "shite", and generally getting myself a reputation for being cheeky. I began off by reading History, but switched to English Literature, influenced by a young tutor called Michael Nevin who took time out to read poetry to me. One day we were reading Andrew Marvell's 'The Garden', and it was when he was explaining the lines

"The nectarine and the curious peach
Into my hands themselves do reach"

that I had my Eureka moment. Eng. Lit. has been my passion ever since, and it is entirely appropriate that it was kindled at Campion Hall where, not that long before, Gerard Manley Hopkins had been The Master, though it took a while before I could get to grips with him.

It was long before I could really understand them, however, that I started going to see Shakespeare's plays, both at Stratford-upon-

Avon and in London, and I remember one early occasion when I was so far up in the Gods I couldn't really see him, I was at Laurence Olivier's *Titus Andronicus*, a performance which was also attended by Sir Winston Churchill, who was mobbed as we all went out. I had a wonderful teacher at Oxford in Mrs. Dorothy Bednarowska who oversaw me from St. Hilda's, and suggested, after I got my B.A. that I should stay on and do a B.Litt. I was in no hurry to leave Oxford, which, apart from the dampness of the weather, I had come to love, and so I went to Lincoln College to work on Jacobean Drama, the result of which now reposes somewhere in the vastness of the Bodleian.

I remained in Oxford for seven years, but had started writing theatre reviews for the undergraduate magazines *Isis* and *Cherwell*, and one day Sheridan Morley told me I should do some, as he did, for the *Times Educational Supplement*. This was how I came to London and got my first job under Walter James, the long time Editor of the *TES*, and met a group of other talented friends among them Wagnerian scholar Patrick Carnegy, now Earl of North Usk, Architectural expert Simon Jenkins, now Sir Simon and eminent fellow theatre critic Michael Billington, CBE. We all met recently in Windsor at the funeral of Walter James, who died at the age of 103.

But I think the moment I realised that I was really here, in England, was the day when my mother and I were in a half full cinema watching Laurence Olivier's newly released film: *Richard III*. This, of course brought back memories of that extraordinary moment in Budapest when the entire audience rose in recognition of their plight, but now, when we got to the Scrivener reading out Hastings' testimony we were surrounded by people eating popcorn, snogging, or falling asleep. They were more amused than horrified at Richard's wickedness. It was five hundred years since they had had to worry about Tyranny or Despotism – they were watching History. I was in a democratic country, I could become an Englishman, and get on with the rest of my life.

LAURENCE OLIVIER
AS RICHARD III

(ONE OF MY FAVOURITE ROLES)
Gerald Scarfe

Appendix

Extracts from some of John Peter's *Sunday Times* reviews of productions of *Richard III*.

1) The point about Richard is that he is not only a vicious psychopathic joker but also a great prince. The best Richards I have seen (Olivier, Ian Holm, Antony Sher, Simon Russell Beale) were great partly because they showed you both the sick killer and the man who was born to command.

2) Enter Robert Lindsay, one of those actors who can command a large audience with the whites of his eyes or a slight pursing of his mouth, and here he takes over the stage at once like a natural conqueror. His Richard is a trickster who takes you into his confidence. It is a powerful beginning. Lindsay is laying the foundations of a character, the earliest fully achieved character in Shakespeare, and this includes the perception that a certain type of criminality thrives on exhibitionism.

Sunday Times, 1st November 1998.

3)   Kenneth   Branagh's   brilliantly   brutish performance, both human and animal, is rooted in the perception that Richard is, first and foremost, an actor. If he has an identity at all, it is that of the expert performer who revels in his own disguises.

4) This is an historic occasion. The new Richard III explodes on the Stratford stage like a thunderclap. The black figure of Antony Sher stands spotlit in the central archway of Willian Dudley's superb white Gothic screen and begins the opening speech in a tone of complacent satisfaction. Sher reveals a pair of black crutches and heaves his wiry, humped body violently forward like a giant malevolent tarantula. From this moment on we are spellbound...the vicious strength is controlled by an agile mind.

Sunday Times 24th June 1984

5) Simon Russell Beale's mesmerising Richard III for the RSC is a prurient sadist of the imagination, a smug, preening actor giving

a private performance for his own enjoyment, which the audience is privileged to overhear.

Sunday Times 13th December 1992

6) Barrie Rutter's idea is to play Richard III as a Yorkshire play in Yorkshire accents, But…to hear Richard say he is "scarce half made oop" or that he will 'stoody fashions to adorn me boody" adds nothing either to him or to Shakespeare.

Sunday Times 13th December 1992

7) The one reason to see this production of *Richard III* is Derek Jacobi's Richard: a black, weasel-like villain whose disability gives him a strange rocking walk, both insinuating and sinister… His humour is savage and contemptuous. In the final scene, his sardonic laugh at his own end almost chills the blood.

8) This is a ridiculous production. I did wonder about the Globe's idea of having all the parts played by women, but nothing prepared me for the sheer amateurishness, the endless, high-

octane ranting or the inept groupings and movement of Barry Kyle's production.

9) Michael Boyd's production is a bit of a disappointment. Richard is a complex character but Aidan McArdle plays him as much more Tricky Dicky than the hound of hell.

10) Brian Cox opens the summer season at Regent's Park with an extremely, I may almost say, ostentatiously dreary production... why does Richard arrive wearing little more than a jockstrap and get dressed during his opening speech? My favourite moment was when a shaven-headed Duke of Buckingham comes on and says "My hair does stand on end to hear her curses". It brings the house down.

Sunday Times June 11th 1995